F-15 EAGLES

BY DENNY VON FINN

BELLWETHER MEDIA · MINNEAPOLIS, MN

EPIC

EPIC BOOKS are no ordinary books. They burst with intense action, high-speed heroics, and shadows of the unknown. Are you ready for an Epic adventure?

This edition first published in 2014 by Bellwether Media, Inc.

No part of this publication may be reproduced in whole or in part without written permission of the publisher. For information regarding permission, write to Bellwether Media, Inc., Attention: Permissions Department, 5357 Penn Avenue South, Minneapolis, MN 55419.

Library of Congress Cataloging-in-Publication Data

Von Finn, Denny.
F-15 Eagles / by Denny Von Finn.
    pages cm. – (Epic: military vehicles)
Includes bibliographical references and index.
 Summary: "Engaging images accompany information about F-15 Eagles. The combination of high-interest subject matter and light text is intended for students in grades 2 through 7"–Provided by publisher.
 Audience: Ages 6-12.
 ISBN 978-1-60014-942-9 (hbk. : alk. paper)
 1. Eagle (Jet fighter plane)–Juvenile literature. I. Title.
UG1242.F5V6525 2014
623.74'64–dc23
                                                        2013002355

Printed in the United States of America, North Mankato, MN.

The photographs in this book are reproduced through the courtesy of the United States Department of Defense. A special thanks to the following for additional photos: Chen Ws, pp. 8, 16; Eugene Berman, p. 17.

TABLE OF CONTENTS

F-15 EAGLES

Two U.S. Air Force pilots patrol the skies in their F-15 Eagles. The jet fighters fly high above a desert. Suddenly their **radar** warns them of danger.

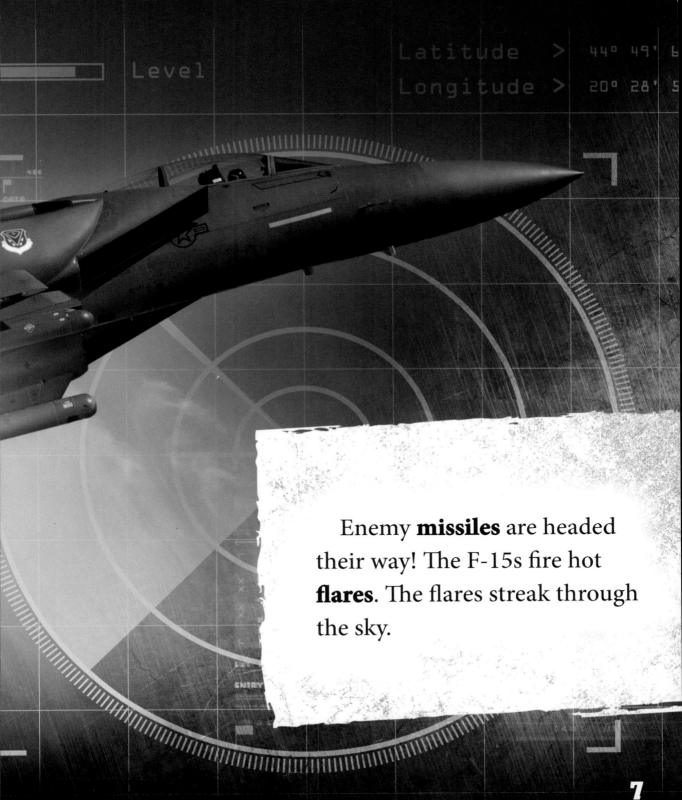

Enemy **missiles** are headed their way! The F-15s fire hot **flares**. The flares streak through the sky.

Range ├┼┼┼┤ ├┼┼┼┤ 100

0

THREAT DETECTED

The enemy missiles follow the flares. The **countermeasures** have worked! Now the F-15s will hunt the aircraft that shot the missiles.

WEAPONS AND FEATURES

MISSILE

BOMB

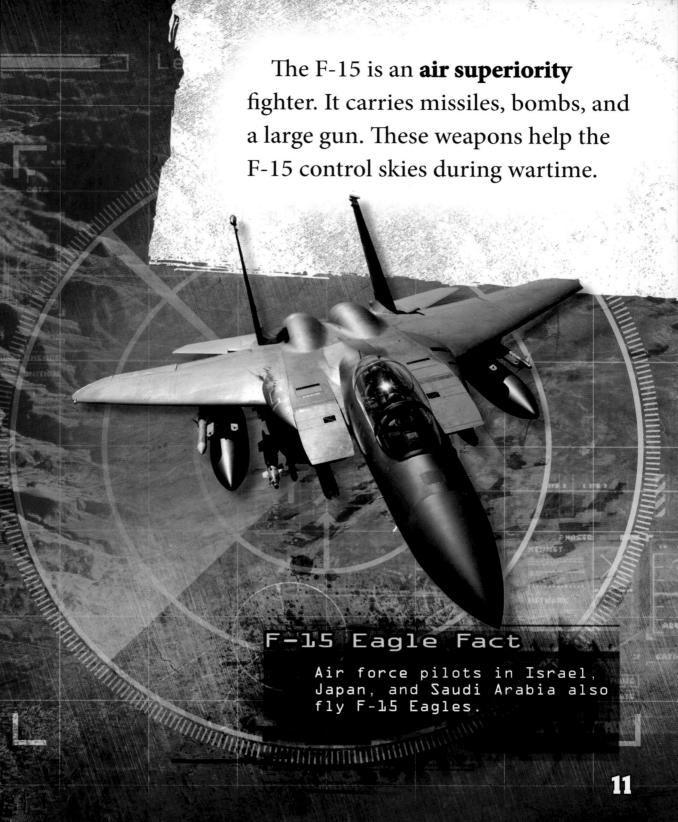

The F-15 is an **air superiority** fighter. It carries missiles, bombs, and a large gun. These weapons help the F-15 control skies during wartime.

F-15 Eagle Fact

Air force pilots in Israel, Japan, and Saudi Arabia also fly F-15 Eagles.

JET ENGINES

Two **jet engines** help the F-15 fly more than twice the speed of sound. This is called **supersonic** flight. F-15s fly much slower during battle.

FUEL TANK

QG

1695

F-15 Eagle Fact

Some F-15s carry extra fuel
tanks under their wings.
Pilots can drop these tanks
when they are empty.

An F-15 pilot tracks enemies on a **head-up display (HUD)**. The pilot fires weapons with a **control stick**.

Range

HUD

F-15 Eagle Fact

The HUD is at eye level.
A pilot can read the HUD
without looking away
from the sky.

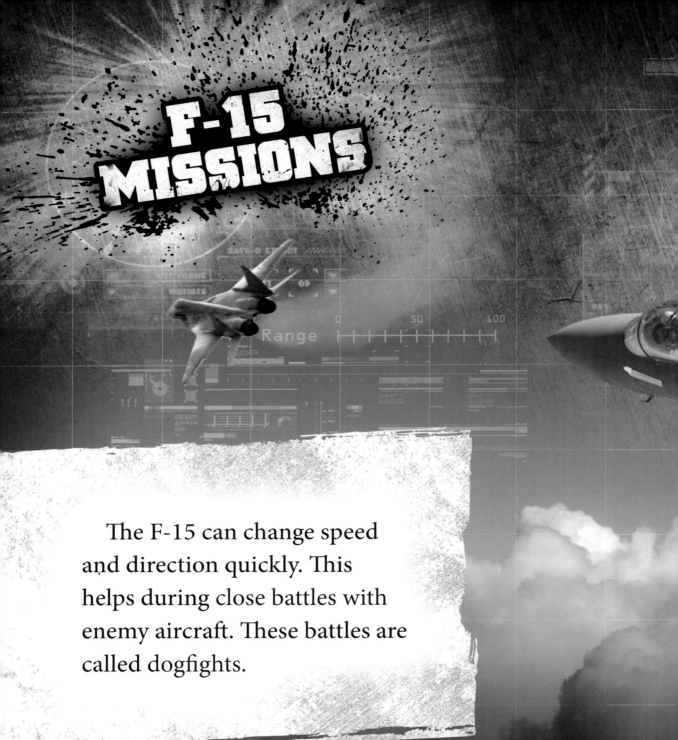

F-15 MISSIONS

The F-15 can change speed and direction quickly. This helps during close battles with enemy aircraft. These battles are called dogfights.

F-15 Eagle Fact

F-15s have won more than 100 close battles. They have never lost a dogfight!

17

The F-15's **avionics** help pilots during their **missions**. These electronics track enemies. They can even guide weapons to enemy targets.

THREAT DETECTED

Level

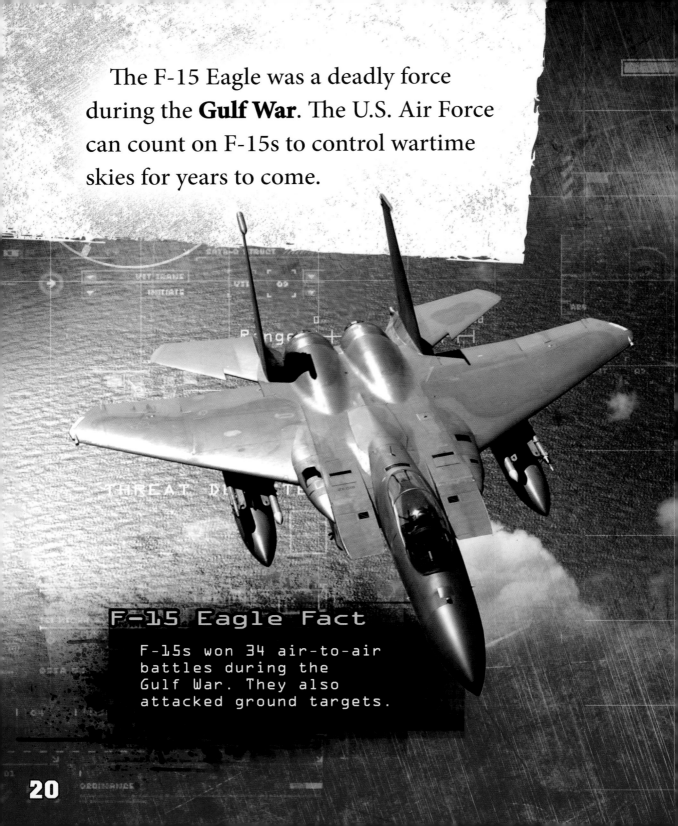

The F-15 Eagle was a deadly force during the **Gulf War**. The U.S. Air Force can count on F-15s to control wartime skies for years to come.

F-15 Eagle Fact

F-15s won 34 air-to-air battles during the Gulf War. They also attacked ground targets.

VEHICLE BREAKDOWN: F-15 EAGLE

Used By:	U.S. Air Force
Entered Service:	1976
Length:	63 feet, 9 inches (19.4 meters)
Height:	18 feet, 6 inches (5.6 meters)
Maximum Takeoff Weight:	68,000 pounds (30,844 kilograms)
Wingspan:	42 feet, 10 inches (13 meters)
Top Speed:	1,875 miles (3,018 kilometers) per hour
Range:	3,450 miles (5,552 kilometers)
Ceiling:	65,000 feet (19,812 meters)
Crew:	1 or 2
Weapons:	gun, missiles, bombs
Primary Mission:	air superiority

GLOSSARY

air superiority—control of the skies during war

avionics—advanced electronics that control an aircraft's radar and weapons

control stick—a joystick that the pilot uses to fly the aircraft and fire weapons

countermeasures—tools an aircraft uses to help it escape enemy fire

flares—hot countermeasures dropped from an aircraft to confuse enemy missiles

Gulf War—a conflict from 1990 to 1991 in which 34 nations fought against Iraq; the war began after Iraq invaded the small country of Kuwait.

head-up display (HUD)—a clear glass screen that displays information in front of a pilot

jet engines—powerful engines that push a plane forward

missiles—explosives that are guided to a target

missions—military tasks

radar—a system that uses radio waves to locate targets

supersonic—faster than the speed of sound; sound travels about 760 miles (1,225 kilometers) per hour at sea level

TO LEARN MORE

At the Library

David, Jack. *F-15 Eagles*. Minneapolis, Minn.: Bellwether Media, 2009.

Von Finn, Denny. *Supersonic Jets*. Minneapolis, Minn.: Bellwether Media, 2010.

Zuehlke, Jeffrey. *Fighter Planes*. Minneapolis, Minn.: Lerner Publications, 2005.

On the Web

Learning more about F-15 Eagles is as easy as 1, 2, 3.

1. Go to www.factsurfer.com.

2. Enter "F-15 Eagles" into the search box.

3. Click the "Surf" button and you will see a list of related Web sites.

With factsurfer.com, finding more information is just a click away.

INDEX